I0428905

In memory of P. Hallus

Copyright © 2016 J.A.W

All rights reserved.

ISBN: 1523696737

ISBN-13: 978-1523696734

Feminism

From the Male Gaze

By J.A.W

Motionless Movement

If you're a man, then to criticize feminism is to be labeled a woman-hating, chauvinistic misogynist. And I'm alright with that. These words have long lost their sting, seeing as how simply disagreeing with anything even remotely female-related can brand you as "anti-woman" these days. If you need it spelled out for you, I am a man, who had begun taking a serious look at modern feminism, only to develop a morbid fascination with it. Not with feminist theory, but with feminist behavior. I noticed from the start that something uniquely screwy was happening. Feminists said, "Educate yourself." So I tried.

As I **listened** and **believed**, I laughed and learned to love the bruises I earned tumbling down the rabbit hole.

There are many books explaining modern feminism, but this is THE BOOK. I wrote THE BOOK, so pepper your angus.

For the first few decades of the feminist movement, it stuck to the tried-and-true guns of free speech, with aspects seeming both necessary and important, minus the crazed man-hating that came from those early periods(tee-hee). In the past few decades however, western feminism has become a loud, outdated, rather ugly movement of lies, hypocrisies, double-standards and utter nonsense. Feminists are quick to tell whoever they can that feminism means "equality for all," even when faced with evidence to the contrary. What's worse is that any time feminists lash out in a universally moronic way, the No True Scotsman fallacy echoes from every hilltop as we're all told "those aren't really feminists."

We live in a time where numerous women claim that western countries are under a "patriarchy" and a "rape culture," yet we all got to watch nearly every major feminist figurehead dance around the subject of the sexual assault which took place in Cologne on New Year's Eve (thanks to intersectional feminism for creating a framework to judge oppression based on race and gender – which is totally not racist or sexist, y'all.)

We even got to witness the female mayor of Cologne suggest women stay an arm's length away from men to avoid being assaulted; the sort of thing feminists would tell you to never say.

If you ever want proof that feminists are hypocrites, just watch them. They want to end "slut shaming," and want the right to show their <u>breasts</u> in public, but then turn around and cry foul at "#shirtgate," when a male scientist wears a shirt depicting pulpy pinups of sword-wielding, scantily-clad, large-<u>breasted</u> women.

They tell us that men don't care about violence against women, then adopt the hashtag "killallmen." When criticized for the violence against men, they called it a "<u>joke</u> hashtag," and said we "<u>shouldn't take jokes seriously.</u>" Then another male scientist makes a <u>joke</u> about women in laboratories, and feminists successfully campaign to have him removed for it.

On any given week, we can all glance at the news and find something that either "outraged" or "offended" feminists. It could be a piece of clothing, a piece of literature, a joke, a video game, a TV show, a comedy sketch, an opinion or even a comic book cover. Their indignation is almost always absurd, and for some reason pointed toward either <u>words,</u> <u>fashion</u> or <u>fiction,</u> but this rage seems seldom aimed at action. We hear that overly-domineering men are examples of "toxic masculinity" that must be done away with, and then Fifty Shades of Grey becomes a best-selling novel.

I'm done pretending that this current form of feminism still has a point in the western world.

You see, some time in the mid-90's, feminism became a hive mind. This hive then proceeded to lose its' mind. Gender studies became Women's studies, single mothers became heroes just for being single, and divorced fathers became vending machines. Women became "strong and independent," whilst also needing legal safety-nets that do not exist for men. When men even suggest that such safety-nets should extend to males as well, feminists (people who advocate for equality between the genders) are swift to say that Men's Rights is a joke.

Women nowadays "don't need no man," but sure as hell seem to need his money, support, protection, employment quotas, female-only college grants and discount incentives for female-run businesses. Point this out, as a man, and you will be called a sexist. Somehow, we're now seeing phrases such as "hegemonic masculinity" and "patriarchy hurts men too," and sadly, people who use such phrases expect to be taken seriously. Call me old-fashioned, but the logic of "men doing things for the sake of men is bad for men" does not compute.

Modern feminism has only one weapon, and that weapon is language, yet in an irony lost on them, they have tried to ban words; "Bossy" being a prominent example. In order to understand about ninety percent of the blithering, barbigerous, buffarilla-like husk that is modern feminism, look no further than our main topic, the progress-less "progressive" elephant in the room.

From here on, it's turtles all the way down.

Social Justice 101

Have you, dearest reader, ever seen or heard someone using the term "SJW" (Social Justice Warrior) as an insult? People normally stumble across this term when casually browsing online nowadays. However, there's no need to worry if it's completely new to you. Rejoice, in fact. People don't usually get a grasp of this subject when first discovering it, so in order to avoid becoming bogged down with information, I have structured this chapter in a very short and specific manner.

You might laugh, and soon see why.

The uninitiated will probably be wondering about the meaning of "Social Justice," as well as its relevance to feminism's current incarnation, right? Well, in the U.S, numerous polls reported finding that approximately eighty percent of Americans do **not** consider themselves to be feminists. Predictably, this was followed by a flood of op-eds, articles, news stories and blog dumpings about this strange "aversion to the F word," all looking for possible answers as to why so few people identify with feminism. The answer, in simple terms, is because of what feminism has allied itself with.

The three following pages will most likely appear to be patronizing, but there's a point to what's next. Indulge me. The answers and their explanations that I'm guiding you towards are at the end of a long, dark, twisted path. So let's take it in stride.

We'll begin with a story. 'The Parable of a Parasite':

One day, a little girl was playing hide-and-seek with her friends in the forest. But the little girl wandered too far, and became lost. She was not able to retrace her steps and could not see or hear her friends, no matter how she shouted or where she looked. At first, she was happy, because she had clearly won the game. But her friends weren't anywhere, it seemed. And so, the little girl began to cry, feeling sad because she was all alone. Suddenly, a tiny little voice spoke to her.

"Hello," said the voice.

"Hello," she replied.

It was a slimy, tiny snail, sparkling with many bright colors as if to attract attention. The snail smiled and asked, "Are you lost? Do you need help?"

"Yes," she said to the snail. "Have you seen my friends? I do not know where to go."

"I have seen them, of course. But I need your help, too," the snail explained. "If you pick me up, and put me in your ear, I will whisper where your friends are."

"Eww," she said. "Why?"

The snail **laughed**, and then told her why. "Because I move awfully slow, and I can not go far by myself. But with *your* legs, I could go very far indeed..."

The little girl did not want a snail in her ear, but if she did not help the snail, then she would stay lost in the forest without her friends.

"Oh, alright," she said to the snail. "But after three steps, you have to get out of my ear. Promise?"

The snail smiled and agreed. "I promise!"

And so, the little girl picked it up and put it beside her head for a moment, letting the tiny snail wiggle out of its shell, and into her ear. Then she took three great, big steps.

"Done," she said.

"Thank you very much," replied the snail, whispering from inside her ear. "To find all of your friends again, just go past the tall, red trees. That is where they are waiting."

This made her very happy. She started to walk, but the snail did not come out of her ear.

"Hey... C'mon, Snail." she said. "You promised to leave."

"I will not keep my promise," the snail explained. "I lied to you, and I will not leave. Now I am in the very back of your ear, and I am so tiny that you can't pull me out. Whenever I whisper, you will have to listen..."

"Why?" asked the girl. "Why did you lie?"

The snail **laughed**, and then told her why. "Because I move awfully slow, and I cannot go far by myself. **But with *your* legs, I could go very far indeed...**"

That concludes 'The Parable of a Parasite.'

It's a hard picture to paint, but that parable puts us exactly where we want to be. And, of course, you already figured it out. The little girl is feminism. The snail is Social Justice. This ideology is parasitic in its very nature; rife with destructive tactics, possessing the worst tendencies from both left-wing radicals and dictatorial states.

Social Justice had latched onto the feminist movement out of pure necessity, because without a host, this parasite dies. Likewise, feminism was lost, and put too much trust in something that it would otherwise avoid. Mirroring the parable's snail, Social Justice Warriors will talk to their potential hosts, and convince them that they are polite, helpful, or politically useful in one way or another. Basically, they need <u>you</u> to buy into their bullshit. They can't get in unless <u>you</u> open the door.

SJWs, in their own words, will declare that the "Social Justice" ideology is synonymous with "justice for all in society." The reason they say this is so that people who disagree with them can be called an enemy of "justice." Also, since societies are comprised of people, they can pick out any group within that society, and declair their critics as enemy of that group. Yes, you read that correctly. And yes, that is the explanation for why SJWs and modern feminists relentlessly call everyone and everything racist, sexist, homophobic, transphobic, misogynistic, and so on.

This means exactly what you'd suspect. Simply *saying* that you are opposed to the ideology of Social Justice enables SJWs to assert that you oppose "justice" for "(_____.)" That blank space will always be women, minorities, gays, lesbians, trans, and any combination thereof.

Without a protected group to hide behind, Social Justice doesn't get very far on its own. They may only claim to empower you as long as you seem to be powerless. Their strength comes from your perceived weakness, and the defending thereof. The worse off that society thinks you are, the more noble your defenders can appear. Plus, with the resources of feminism and the benefit of calling critics misogynistic... they could go very far indeed.

Progressing a Regression

Now, that brief introduction to Social Justice should have given you a good idea about their involvement, **but we haven't even touched on their beliefs yet.** So, in order to fully understand the actions of SJWs, I'll parrot/paraphrase the most succinct explanation of their views that I've ever heard. This will start to give you some insight into what happened to feminism.

Social Justice calls for "equality of <u>outcome</u>," and not "equality of <u>opportunity</u>." Some have tried to use more favorable language, but also while keeping the ideology tied to "corrective justice" or "distributive justice." Some of them now take it as far as "racial justice." And again, justice to them is outcome, not opportunity. In essence, if I were of a similar mind to such people, then I would walk into a family reunion in rural Kentucky and become very upset and "worried" by the "problematic" lack of minority representation, and I would probably be outraged if the family had more sons than daughters. "Too many white men, not enough (insert group here)."

Their lines of reasoning often have no reasons behind them, just excuses meant to justify the means. Once you're aware that Social Justice has been influencing modern feminism, you'll be able to spot the consequences. Feminism calls for equality. Social Justice calls for its own idea of equality, and does so under the guise of feminism.

How do you tell the difference, then? An easy way to determine if you're hearing/reading something from an "equality feminist," or a "Social Justice feminist" is to swap the genders on what they're telling you.

"We need more men in nursing and we need more male teachers, since female-dominated fields show the inequality in our culture." That kind of crap. Might as well say that more policewomen need to be shot every year, since men dominate that as well. While we're at it, too many women work in Women's Studies...

Naturally, you won't hear people complaining about those things, but if men dominate any field, we start to see news articles about the "problematic" male presence in particular careers, and start reading about "boy's clubs." This is Social Justice Feminism in action.

Next time somebody bitches endlessly about "too many men in ____," take note of who's yapping: Bloggers, columnists, reporters, and other people who are unqualified for the very careers they complain about. And the one thing they have in common are their attempts at large-scale communication. Why spend time talking to one potential host when you could reach thousands?

"If you're a woman, and think that the STEM fields need more women, then why not get a STEM job?"

The only person you would need to ask such a thing is either an idiot, or a Social Justice feminist. We rarely hear women with such positions even mentioning how many men they work with, yet we've got quite a number of SJW types, who have nothing to do with the fields perturbing them, constantly yammering on about injustice and inequality. They often cite words or early-life influences for why there are not more women in these occupations, and blame our culture at large for discouraging young girls by telling them what kind of jobs women should have; while acting as though they are not members of our culture. And again, in the typical fashion of SJW double-think, they presume to tell women what to do with their lives, based solely upon their dislike of seeing more men doing a particular thing. Equality, folks...

Their idea of "helping" to solve these "problems" is to complain, because they can't get very far on their own. It's up to other people to make accomplishments, as they shout behind the shield of women and minorities.

Social Justice Warriors are essentially trying to be Orwellian Big Brothers, and that is far from hyperbole. Through the steady creation of their very own Social Justice Newspeak, many declare that racism against whites is not possible, since anti-white rhetoric is in the category of "punching up" rather than "punching down." Punching up is to resist oppressors, and punching down is to oppress.

When SJWs aren't busy dreaming up categories that distinguish between what kind of racism they allow and what kind they forbid, these dingbats are changing words in order to further suit their ideological demands.

"Racism = prejudice + power."

If that looks at all familiar, it's because SJWs instinctively say, type, tweet and blog it whenever they get the chance. If you even slightly suggest that racial prejudice or discrimination is racist no matter the race, SJWs will "correct" you with their new definition. As far as they're concerned, minorities who hate whites are, by definition, not capable of racism.

Whites are always the majority to them, since they don't concern themselves with facts, such as, let's say... global population. Oddly enough, these self-proclaimed crusaders against sexist and racist views are very fond of telling everyone how powerless women and minorities are. What kind of power? The power kind of power. You name it, and SJWs will say only straight white men have it, so if you're not a hetero white dude, they will endlessly fight to free you from your wretched existence. Misandry (hatred of men) is also considered to be something that simply cannot exist for the same kind of "reasoning." You may have already seen a well known sentence from Robin Morgan that expresses this view. I'm going to quote it. Please pay special attention to the wording.

"I feel that 'man-hating' is an honorable and viable political act, that the oppressed have a right to class-hatred against the class that is oppressing them." - Robin Morgan.

Removing the implications of economic and social status from the word "class" and repurposing it to describe an entire sex looks exactly like what it is: Malicious wordplay. When men become a "class" and stop being "people," then "man-hating" is no longer the hatred of people. It's a political act.

By twisting words in this fashion, they paint their own prejudice as anything but prejudice.

And this is just the start of how they try to police language so it conforms to the thoughts that they alone can approve. Strap in, kiddos, the fuckery has only just begun.

In response to the statement, "while sexism exists, not all men are the perpetrators," one twitter user posted the following: "Lies. ALL MEN benefit from patriarchy. **Privilege IS oppression**."

This is one of their main labeling strategies. In their minds, being better off than anyone else makes you an oppressor of one group or another. Even if you are not actually better off. To them, by the virtue of being categorized as one thing, you oppress another. If you are male, you probably oppress women. If you are white, you probably oppress minorities. If you are straight, you probably oppress gays. If you are "cisgendered," then you are probably transphobic.

If you are a heterosexual, cisgendered white

man... good luck. They really don't like you people. And should you choose to reject any label they put on you, you will be asked how you "support" or "help" or "contribute to" (insert group here).

No answer given to SJWs can be satisfactory, and for all the wrong reasons.

Due to the very terms they use, if you are straight and support gay rights, you're still in the wrong because other heterosexuals did/do not in the past/present, or you benefit from "straight privilege". No matter what you've done, it isn't enough. The reason why this strategy is so widely employed in the media they've infected is because it successfully makes several implications while using only a small number of words. It also gives Social Justice Warriors a verbal escape route, allowing them the option to paint anyone they deem "privileged" as an oppressor or a _____-ist/-phobe, to avoid topics or addressing arguments.

They are Thought Police who all speak and write with a very specific vocabulary that compliments their carefully crafted vernacular; one filled with statements designed to be reinforced and reused. The reason why is simple.

By mixing their definitions of racism, power, privilege and oppression, they swiftly create linguistic Kafkatraps (Google that). How they are going to respond to any answer you give them depends solely on how they want to label you.

SJWs do not want a debate. They do not want open dialogue. They do not want an argument. They especially do not want any facts you bring them. They want a racist, a sexist, a misogynist, a bigot, a homophobe or a transphobe. They want an enemy with a bad label, because if a collective of "progressive" people are calling you any of those things, they elevate themselves by comparison. Would an onlooker consider viewing things from the side of a racist, bigoted, privileged man-child that hates women? If somebody does come to your defense, they will be seen as a supporter of racism or sexism or whatever label they've repeated and imposed.

Anyone who agrees with you instead of Social Justice is automatically cast in the same bad light. And if more than one person supports you and not them, then SJWs will claim that a mob of ravenous, bigoted, sexist, homophobic racists are harassing them because they hate (insert group here.) Also, when they shout-down or even physically block people from speaking... it's not "censorship." They call it "no-platforming." When I alluded to Orwell's 1984, I wasn't fuckin' kidding.

This is their way.

They will start by claiming to be oppressed or censored in some regard or another, then they will crusade to censor and control others.

Whenever they can, SJWs will advocate or implement measures against Freedom of Speech, even on the microscale. Disagreement will be blocked, banned, or the speaker will be slandered through the labeling tactics I've described, all under the guise of "stopping hate-speech." Even other feminists have been victims of the SJW mob-mentality.

When Christina Marie Hoff Sommers, who is a philosophy teacher, (equality) feminist and total milf, began voicing her concerns about odd double-standards and twisted logic becoming the norm, SJ-feminists were quick to call her everything they could get away with. And they got away with a lot. "Female impersonator," "Rape-apologist," "Anti-woman," "Traitor to her gender," and so on. What brought this about? She wrote a book, titled "Who Stole Feminism?" Her book was a plea for moderation, and SJ-feminists responded with various degrees of extremism. New-age college students have protested Sommers' speeches without ever having read a word she has written. When she questions something, she is called "hateful." When she disapproves of something, her views are called "harmful" or "problematic." When she is scheduled to speak to a college classroom, Social Justice feminism groups on campus create "safe spaces" where people can go to hear music and drink tea and hot chocolate, sparing their ears from the injustice of questions raised by a mild-mannered sixty year old woman.

When she criticized the government-mandated establishment of kangaroo courts instead of law-enforcement to investigate college sexual assault, she became "pro-rape" in their eyes; because "fuck the police," I guess. When she brings up example after example of false rape claims on college campuses, where the woman was proven to be lying, yet the accused man is still expelled, she again is called "pro-rape."

Christina could have easily avoided running afoul with these people if she simply hadn't remained a feminist who still believes that feminism means "equality for all." She even teamed up with the American Enterprise Institute and created a video series called the "Factual Feminist." Presumably because the latter does not imply the former these days.

When SJWs invaded feminism, they were able to take it over with relative ease due to the movement's nature. To clarify, every pore of Social Justice oozes with a mental diarrhea known as Postmodern Theory. Objectivity is not nor has ever been a virtue to them, and evidence is either ignored or fabricated.

For instance, who remembers the (now deleted) video entitled "Drunk Girl In Public" by Stephen Zhang? On November 11th, 2014, this video went viral for showing a drunk girl approaching strangers and acting lost and confused. All of the men she approached tried to take her home, presumably to take advantage of her. Feminists and SJWs alike were outraged over how evil and sexist men are, and shouted from the hills about how they were right all along.

Then the truth came out. This video was a hoax, where it seemed nobody knew the true intentions of it, save for the directors, Stephen Zhang and Seth Leach. The "Drunk Girl" was an actress named Jennifer Box, who was led to believe that she was just taking part in a fake prank video – typical of YouTube's idea of entertainment – while all of the men were random guys that were asked if they would appear in a quick scene for a student film, who the actress later referred to as "nothing but perfect gentlemen." As I said, this video went viral, and less than a week later, some of those men found it online.

When one of them took to Facebook and expressed his well-placed anger for having been portrayed as a rapist in the video, Seth Leach replied to him in an... unusual manner.

"*Yo dude, totally cool with you telling everyone that we came up to you and you acted the part for the video. We deal with these situations, all the time. The important thing to consider, is that this video is going to get you well known and have a future with us and our company. We need to hang out soon, cause drinks are on me all night. We are going to be huge and you are apart of it. Just go with it dude, you are in our team now and we will take care of you.*" - Seth Leach.

Portrays a man as a rapist, then says hes part of the team... Stay classy, Seth.

These people could be considered to be an unsuccessful example of Social Justice Warriors attempting to pander and bait feminists into accepting them, but keep in mind that when their video was popular, it was monetized with ads. Somebody got paid for this.

Others have garnered more success, such as the folks who produced the "10 Hours of Walking in NYC as a Woman" video. At the time of writing, this is the only video on this particular YouTube channel, and the channel name is "Street HarassmentVideo." They know what they're doing, and yes, the video has ads.

This is one of numerous ways that Social Justice Warriors use sensationalist media tactics to slip into the ranks of feminism, arriving within a Trojan Horse to spur feminists on with stories of damsels in distress. Problem is, when feminists see these distressed damsels, they start making calls to action, rather than taking any actual actions.

Basically, women are strong, independent, and don't need no man. So man up and go save them.

Victim Narrative

Whenever women are shown in anyway to be oppressed, harassed, victimized or treated badly in some regard or another, no matter how small the slight, feminism will be there to express outrage and offense. However, feminists need content to be outraged at, and this is where Social Justice Warriors have them covered.

SJW activists never miss the opportunity to gain influence, typically by clinging onto a preexisting movement, such as BlackLivesMatter. I had intended to carefully address the BLM movement, but I won't address it at all, because I remembered cats don't bark and niggas don't read. Anyway, YouTube, Twitter and Tumblr are breeding grounds for these would-be modern leaders of Social Justice-infused civil rights, doing whatever they can to attach their names to a political buzz or recent event. In the internet age, one tactic reigns supreme: Click Bait.

These SJW "activists" and "taste makers" create things that legions of folks will click on, and they employ all of the modern click-bait tactics; "...as a woman," "...girl in public," "...epidemic," "every day harassment at..." etc. A very small minority of Social Justice Warriors report/invent/spread something about massive injustices, collect ad revenue from people who haven't figured out what AdBlock is, and then silently slink back to where they crawled from, leaving Social Justice feminists shouting at everyone, while equality feminists try to pick up the pieces.

Instead of picking up those pieces and correcting the skewed or outright false information, however, a portion of feminists will fall for it. When feminists get drummed up about sexism, then get told that 80% of Americans aren't feminists, they feel like their friends are all gone, and only the snail can help.

SJW profiteers have been creating more SJWs, spawning them from modern feminism's easily exploitable culture of complaints.

Everything becomes sexist, because there's money in making a bunch of videos about sexism in all fields and subcultures, be it comic books, TV, games, movies, advertising or who knows what's next. If a woman is called a bitch on the internet, she is a victim of online harassment, and need only express sadness, outrage, fear or a general puppy-dog, doe-eyed demeanor in order to start getting donations through Patreon.

Some women make upwards of six-thousand dollars a month in donations for having their feelings hurt, and even putting it this way can earn you criticism for "harassing a victim of online harassment." Well, Trigger Warning: My fuck-barrel is officially depleted, and there are none left to give. As a side-note, the next time you see a popular video pushing the narrative of "all women/minorities are victims," dig around and I'll bet there's either a biased media company, viral-video agency or lone SJW with a Patreon page behind it.

Unsurprisingly, when folks claim allegiance with feminism, they're let in. SJWs are no exception, even when they treat women like complete dipshits.

Consider the following:

"Jake was drunk. Josie was drunk. Jake and Josie **hooked up**. Josie could not consent. The next day, Jake was charged with **rape**. A woman who is intoxicated cannot give her legal consent for **sex**, so proceeding under these circumstances is a crime. It only takes a single day to ruin your life."

Honestly, think about the quote above. I did not make it up. This text was taken from an anti-rape poster designed to discourage college men from engaging in sexual activities with inebriated women.

In the narrative this poster weaves, **both** are drunk, **both** "hooked up," and only the man is responsible for the ensuing intercourse. The woman has no agency in the given scenario. There is only one message to take away from this: "Drunk men are smarter and more capable than drunk women."

If you disagree, then what else is being said here? Is it "Guys, avoid drunk women, they'll agree to sex, then sober up and accuse you of rape"? By this logic, a man and a woman who have equal amounts of wine during a date means that any sex afterwards is rape – planned and perpetrated by the man. If "feminism is about equality," then imagine if the opposite was said. Once you imagine it, then you'll know it was the Social Justice branch of feminism that cooked it up. The poster would make sense if it said the woman was black-out drunk and was unconscious, but no.

"Jake was drunk. Josie was drunk. Jake and Josie hooked up…"

Some of you will completely miss the point. So when you're done screaming "RAPE APOLOGY," take a breath and pay attention. You need to understand it the most.

In the minds of far too many SJWs and "progressive" feminists, women are children. Women are dumb. Women cannot be held accountable for their actions whenever they interact with men. Women have no agency in their eyes, since they can only be acted upon, and cannot act themselves. They view women as passive objects incapable of choice. If a man and a woman are **both** drunk and have sex, the man is responsible and the woman was taken advantage of, no matter the circumstance.

Now, if you still think I'm defending rape, I'll spell it out again. I'm going to remove the sexual element.

"Jake was drunk. Josie was drunk. Jake and Josie **practiced boxing**. Josie could not consent. The next day, Jake was charged with **assault**. A woman who is intoxicated cannot give her legal consent to **practice boxing**, so proceeding under these circumstances is a crime. It only takes a single day to ruin your life."

They don't want women to be viewed as capable of taking action or making choices. Women must <u>always</u> be seen as a passive object. Men must <u>always</u> act.

They need women to be victims at all times, or else they'd be risking the strength of their criticism-shield. Treating women as active agents gets in the way of their narrative, and it worries me how many feminists seem to see no irony with how Social Justice behaves.

"Women are strong, equal to men, and independent. But don't judge a woman the same way you would judge a man."

"They both had a few drinks, and that means the man raped her. Don't ask her the same questions you asked him though, because that would be blaming the victim."

What if the poster had one, tiny, single change?

"A woman who is intoxicated **<u>may not</u>** give her legal consent..." Write it that way, and she wouldn't be "**<u>allowed</u>**" to make a choice.

"A woman who is intoxicated **<u>cannot</u>** give her legal consent..." Written like that, and she becomes "**<u>unable</u>**" to make a choice.

No matter which way it's worded, the man is held responsible because he is capable and competent. Yet the woman holds no responsibility because she is incapable and incompetent. Does that sound sexist? Well, talk to the Social Justice Warriors, because they're the ones churning this crap out. SJWs need victims, and the language they use is designed to turn women into inane *things* that men misuse.

On the topics of narrative and censorship, feminists and SJWs on the whole do not create much of anything, usually due to lack of talent or competence. Instead, they complain until somebody produces something for them. Feminism used to do things, but Social Justice has been rubbing off on them in all the worst ways. Seriously, name five accomplishments in the last fifteen years made by modern feminism in the west without saying "raise awareness."

The majority are consumers, not creators. Because of this, they advocate either the banning or changing of whatever entertainment product sets off their delicate sensibilities. Can't play as a girl in a particular video game? Then engage in "activism" (yammering on twitter) and "campaign" against the creators (by yammering on twitter). A character in some book get raped? Better yammer again, because how dare a male author put his fictional females through that? Better call him a "rape apologist" so he has to waste his time defending himself from the accusation, instead of calling you dumb for complaining about crimes against fictional characters.

Hilariously, whenever comics, video games, TV shows or movies are tailored to meet their online demands for change, the change is harshly criticized, or if the product itself was planned, created and specifically marketed to them, the product is panned by critics or it just flat-out bombs. This happens most noticeably with video games, since several projects described as "inclusive," "pro-feminist" or "progressive" have tanked. Sometimes they do so poorly that the creators rage-quit the gaming industry altogether. This happens because feminists and Social Justice Warriors complain about something they wouldn't buy due to (insert reason), and even after the creators give in and pander to them, the SJWs still don't purchase it. Surprise, surprise, self-righteous crybabies are fickle.

I won't bother discussing GamerGate, since games are for faggots and faggotry is for queers. However, when people give examples of <u>successful</u> games that are "progressive" or "inclusive" they tend to be games like Dragon Age, where the design choices (to me) seem to follow a checklist.

"Three gay side-characters, check. One or two trans characters, check. Four to eight plot-relevant non-white characters, check. Love-interest characters written to be bisexual, check." Essentially, the sort of games that are packed with so much stuff that the characters within the game will have enough dialogue incorporated to suit whoever the hell is playing it.

I do not fault Bioware (the company behind the Dragon Age series) for taking this approach, since if they have the time/funds to create more content for their games, then more power to them. Instead, I fault Bioware for rushing the

Mass Effect 3 ending, and for making the plots of Dragon Age 2 and 3 boring as shit; not to mention Tali'Zorah's stock photo face. I also find it weird that their games typically follow an "end of the world" story where it's up to the player to save the day, but there's still apparently enough time to find out who's gay, lesbian or transgender...

"Oh my God! Demons/Reapers/Darkspawn are destroying the world! So... if you show me yours, I'll show you mine."

Pacing, Bioware... pacing. And seriously, your company was once attached to Baulder's Gate. What happened to you people? Other than EA.

It was EA, wasn't it?

Unsocial Media

The internet provides safe places to speak about feminism, the rights of men and the relationships between men and women, where we can rationally discuss gender and politics... right? If you think/thought that to be true, then you are/were a colossal moron. No two ways about it. Twitter is where people who have nothing to say go to speak, and Facebook is where the vain go to show how little they matter. If the last two statements offend you, then go write a blog and send out a tweet, because I'll totally, truly, really, really want to read your vapid, pointless nonsense.

The opening paragraph for this section is an example of a trolling tactic that I've come to call "dismissive baiting," where places, discussions, issues, stances or people are painted with a broad brush, then insulted in one way or another. What sets it apart from typical trolling is that the troll dismisses the validity of responses before they even receive any. I tend to find these trolls to be the most entertaining, due to their hit-and-(pretend-to)-run nature, added to the fact that they are often confused for <u>people who actually believe what they write.</u>

The cause of this confusion is that trolls do this on purpose, and enjoy the irony and general butthurt it induces. Feminists and SJWs, on the other hand, have before and will again write something in this way. There will be a statement from them, or more likely, a reaction, followed by claims that those who disagree are sexist, racist or both.

Trolls are everywhere. Show that you have a vested interest in something, and your bias and weakness on the subject will be exploited for the lulz. Take a lesson from Batman: An enemy who fights you for the pure fun of it is the worst you'll ever know, hence "Don't feed the trolls."

Problem is, feminists don't seem to know what trolls eat. For two amazing examples, look no further than "FreeBleeding" and "#EndFathersDay." A woman named Kiran Gandhi ran a marathon on her period, without a tampon, as a feminist statement about the bodies of women in support of "FreeBleeding." The hashtag "EndFathersDay" trended for a while on Twitter, as feminists complained about fathers not deserving a day to celebrate, since there were so many single mothers and that men instigate domestic violence.

Here's where things git gud. Both "FreeBleeding" and "#EndFathersDay" were created by the hacker known as 4chan, who has messed with people from all walks of life. FreeBleeding was conjured with the hope that feminists would take it seriously. The Twitter hashtag "EndFathersDay" was also made to bait feminists into advocating for it. Both of these were successful. Feminists fell for them, once again proving the validity of Poe's Law. All it takes to accomplish this is to look at how Social Justice feminists behave, and then come up with something so stupid that not even they would be able to immediately identify it as a parody of their own beliefs.

So yes, a woman ran a marathon with blood seeping through her pants because 4chan knew a feminist somewhere would be dumb enough to do it. It was an incident which placed nearly 74% of keks in danger of becoming permanently topped, and due to excessive tipping, there are fedoras missing to this very day.

Thanks to how modern feminism now operates as a surrogate force for Social Justice, with their campaigns of "killallmen," "man-spreading" and the general weirdness taking place on Tumblr, trolls see feminists as a fruit that's ripe for the picking. Instead of outright insulting feminism however, trolls play with their reactionary nature by posing as "allies" or "progressives" or just plain run-of-the-mill feminists; the characters Godfrey Elfwick and Anne Gus are among the more blatant examples of this. It is often the case that SJ-feminists cannot tell the difference between themselves and the people fucking with them. That fact alone speaks volumes, and the discovery of trolling plots are often followed by quiet shame from those who fell into their traps. Even the SJW Suey Park (of #CancelColbert infamy) had shown a bit of regret for her reactionary behaviors.

She used to "advocate against racism," but simultaneously wrote things such as "Whiteness will always be the enemy." On the subject of white people, one of my favorite quotes to ever come from her was this:

"Well, one, they won't be the majority for long. And two, I don't want any ally who is going to use my <u>emotional labor</u> with no guarantee of aiding my liberation. And so I feel like this question that white America asks of us, 'Why can't you be reasonable to get us to work with you?' And I keep saying, <u>being reasonable has never worked in history</u>. All other big <u>racial justice</u> movements, all of the big historical figures in <u>racial justice</u> were never reasonable."

More recent things written on her Twitter account seem like night and day. "Reclaiming MY voice. Made the mistake of trusting the loudest voices and let them jerk me around. The wisest voices aren't the loudest." She also wrote, "Why would we want people to live in white guilt? White guilt is an expression of self-hate and never productive."

Even better, "Too tired to engage, but I will say that the violence I have experienced in SJW circles has been greater than that of 'racist trolls'."

She did also go on to say that she was scared of a troll claiming to be a sniper outside of her house... so there goes another fedora.

Strangely, it's through social media that we, as a people, are able to watch the progression, evolution and devolution of different groups. We can track where they start, where they go, and where they eventually end up. I, for one, am not nor have ever been surprised by my generation's actions. This is, in fact, exactly what I expected. You see, people are kind of like Digimon. Atheists become demagogues, cross-dressers become transgender, furries turn into otherkin, tumblrinas turn into fat feminists, and of course, emos and well-to-do special-snowflakes turn into Social Justice Warriors.

When these groups overlap, a lolcow is born, forever enshrined within the annals of Encyclopedia Dramatica.

Feelings ≠ Facts

When feminists say underwear and bikini commercials are too sexualized, do they truly think that advertising bras and panties with attractive models is meant as an insult to larger women? Maybe these advertisements are sexualized so that men are persuaded to purchase bras and panties?

If you put boys on the cover of those oven toys, is that really doing something to/for society? Would changing Barbie's Dream House to Barbie's Chemistry Lab dramatically shift the world, or just be another hunk of Chinese plastic to distract your ugly children with?

I often find myself being completely baffled by the projection feminists seem to have these days, what with their anti-fat-shaming and slut-walking and body image campaigns. Blaming the world at large for how they see themselves is strange to me, but rather than accepting themselves for who they are, or making changes within themselves, they want the perceptions and values of everyone else around them to change. Statistically, in the U.S, damn-near everybody is fat. So while feminists complain about thin female models, the rest of us remain quiet.

Because we're eating.

I know people don't typically like to hear this, but your feelings mean nothing to me. Not because you're a (insert identity), but because I don't know you, and you don't know me. Put simply: Your tears, my dear, mean nothing here.

However, feelings mean even less when you're trying to debate facts. Watch any debate on feminism, and listen to how many times you hear the words "I feel." If you're going to present something as a genuine problem, start with why it's a problem, then support the claim with evidence, not emotions. Feeling something doesn't make it true. Feeling like an underdog doesn't make you an underdog, nor does it make everyone who disagrees with you an enemy.

Far too many feminists and Social Justice Warriors are quick to say <u>sex</u> and <u>race</u> do not matter and should not be taken into consideration, unless they are writing/talking about a subject who happens to be a <u>white</u> <u>male</u>. Never point out this hypocrisy to them, because you will be bombarded by excuses about "historical precedents" and "past/present racial privilege." Engaging with them in this regard has proven time and time again to be a waste of time, seeing as how they rarely possess a sense of personal responsibility. Their own words will be excused as "passionate" or "pent-up frustration due to oppression." This defense is as strong as it is weak, since to disagree further can earn you a label as they try to send you down the rabbit hole of Newspeak.

Here's a bit of information that's totally unrelated to anything. In 2014, it was discovered that shirts with the phrase "This is what a Feminist looks like" were being made in sweatshops by underpaid women in the third world. Oopsy-daisy.

The most effective tool to combat SJ-feminism is ridicule, mockery and humor. Laughter is the best medicine, which explains why women aren't good comedians or doctors.

Glass Standards

"If feminists didn't have double standards, they would have no standards at all." - Unknown

That quote just about sums it up. Double-standards have been present with feminism for all its life, but now with Social Justice in their corner, they've made it clear that equality isn't for everyone. If an issue isn't exclusively about women, feminists won't fight very hard over it. For the simplest example of this, women got voting rights in the 1920's, whereas blacks got voting rights in the mid-1960's. Was feminism responsible for black voting rights, or was it due to a little-known movement called "Civil Rights" perhaps? Feminists love to claim being part of all equality movements, but often have had minimal to no impact on them whatsoever. If only around 18-22% of Americans identify themselves as feminists, why do they always find ways to get credit for accomplishments? Even as recently as the legalization of gay marriage in the U.S, some were quick to call it a "feminist victory." And a number of gays threw hissy fits about it, calling themselves "gays against feminism." Interesting thought, no?

If you do a few easy Google searches, you can find plenty of feminist articles and blogs that are quite blatantly against gay marriage. In 2014, some...body, named Janani Balasubramanian, wrote an article titled *"3 Ways the Gay Rights Agenda™ Has Perpetuated Oppression."* To put it mildly, this article is goddamn-fuckin'-crazy-weird as shit. As far as I can tell, the author of this is about as gay and as feminist as they come, but is horrifyingly steeped in Social Justice. To quote the article directly, with some underlining for emphasis:

"These are supposed to be moments in history that we — those of us who are queer and trans and <u>allies</u> — are supposed to be celebrating. But behind every rainbow flag, there's a pot of Goldman Sachs (and a <u>conservative agenda</u>). Rather than victories, several moments in recent history of the gay movement have been huge losses. The gay rights movement has won rights and recognition that largely serve the interests of <u>white</u>, wealthy <u>cisgender gay men</u> to the detriment of **poor queers** and queer people of color, and to the detriment of <u>racial and economic justice</u> more generally. Again, these are victories for the only most enfranchised gay people. <u>Thus, they are mechanisms for perpetuating injustice.</u>"

After a lot of weird babbling, the article goes on to make a lot of other crazy claims. "Marriage equality may be a victory for gay rights, but it's also a victory for the historically oppressive institution of marriage," among other things about the military industrial complex. As a side note, it's hard not to laugh at progressives and SJWs who use words like "allies" as if they are at war, along with phrases like "people of color" as if to co-opt "colored people." They are against racism, then blame every problem on white people. With folks like this attempting to represent them in written media, "poor queers" indeed...

When SJWs begin to cannibalize each other in the name of Social Justice, you know something is wrong with them. These are not just minor disagreements, there's a whole other way this crap manifests. I have (and so can you) find article after article from big feminist blogs, websites and magazines about how "white feminism" needs to fade away, and that "white-passing people of color" might still have "white privilege." Well, oh golly, gosh, gooseberries and fiddlesticks if that's the case.

"White man" is used pejoratively in many publications, as is "conservative" and "right-wing." For equality movements to speak in this manner without any irony is characteristic of how backwards these progressives are. There is a website known as Everyday Feminism, and I highly recommend reading the insanity that goes on there. Some of my favorite articles are as follows:

"3 Things Privileged White People Should Consider When House-Hunting in Gentrifying Cities." - This reads like a Social Justice version of Star Trek's Prime Directive.

"My Partner Came Out As a Man – And I Struggled With Losing My Lesbian Identity." - An interesting story filled with oddities, but the title broke my funny bone(r).

"From Manspreading to Mansplaining — 6 Ways Men Dominate the Spaces Around Them." - Wish this idiot was joking.

"4 Tired Tropes That Perfectly Explain What Misogynoir Is – And How You Can Stop It." - You're drunk, Shaniqua. Go to sleep.

"6 Strategies for Setting Boundaries with Your Therapist." - How does that make you feel?

"11 Common Ways White Folks Avoid Taking Responsibility for Racism in the US." - This is a white-guilt goldmine.

"Your FitBit Is Ruining Your Relationship with Your Body – Here Are 3 Reasons Why." - Contains the greatest line ever written, "Because it's annoyingly – and exhaustingly – apparent that we live in a world that worships at the altar of health." Oink.

"8 Harmful Examples of Standard American English Privilege." - Hilarious title, boring article.

"Why Affirming the Beauty of Blackness Is Not Same as Putting White People Down." - Didn't know this was an issue. And after reading it, I don't think it ever was.

"Why These Common 'Nice Guy' Behaviors Are Actually Sexist Microaggressions." - To quote Dave Chappelle, "Chivalry is dead, and women killed it."

That's just a small handful, and I once again highly recommend you read through all of those, and then some. Since there are so many different articles from a slew of different authors on Everyday Feminism, you'd be wise to approach each one as its own thing, rather than a streamlined narrative. But I'll hazard a guess and say you'll spot the patterns pretty quick.

The rhetoric, the flaunting of a victim-status and the fabrication of issues is astounding. Some of the articles have interesting points of view, and some seem to stem out of experiences from the pasts of whoever the authors are, but the despising of "whiteness" and men, mixed with Social Justice ideals and Newspeak make for one hell of a witch's brew. The last article in the list, ("*Why These Common 'Nice Guy' Behaviors Are Actually Sexist Microaggressions*") is a perfect summation of their double-standards. The way I see it, when these people categorize "nice guy behaviors" as sexist, then they have lost all right to expect men to be nice to them. Reap what you sow, you sows.

Sargon's Law

"I, an ethnic minority woman, cannot be racist or sexist towards white men, because racism and sexism describe structures of privilege based on race and gender. Therefore, women of colour and minority genders cannot be racist or sexist, since we do not stand to benefit from such a system." - Bahar Mustafa, student union Welfare and Diversity Officer, Goldsmiths University.

"No white–cis–men pls." - Bahar Mustafa, student union Welfare and Diversity Officer, Goldsmiths University.

"8chan, the central hive of #Gamergate, is also an active pedophile network." - Sarah Nyberg.

"I'm attracted to (usually) about 6 to 12. been attracted to as low as 4 but that's atypical." - Sarah Nyberg.

This, is Sargon's Law: *"Whenever a SJW makes a character judgment, that judgment is true about themselves."* - Carl Benjamin, aka Sargon of Akkad.

Shifting gears slightly, but keep that law in mind. Why do people think that SJWs are racist and that feminists hate men? Is it because they're losing a few PR campaigns, or because people are actually judging them on <u>what they say and what they do</u>, rather than <u>what they say they do?</u> I'll leave you to ponder that, based on what you know.

Researching articles, papers and other publications, as well as chatting online with SJWs often leaves me with an odd sensation, as if a pressure valve is perpetually prepared to pop behind my eyes. "Frustrating" is the nearest word to hand, but it's too connotative of a sense of anger. I'm not "mad" about most of what I've seen and read, but suffice it to say that interacting with them leaves me sufficiently "not okay." The phrase "talking to a wall" seems apt, but only if said wall is being smeared with shit by baboons as I continue urging the wall to do something. However, due to my infinite kindness and intrinsically-male sense of fairness, I'll go ahead and extend an olive branch to feminists. There are some legitimately great women still in the world who are trying to keep the feminism brand respectable.

People such as Christina Hoff Sommers (BasedMom), Camille Paglia (JabberJaw incarnate), Liana Kerzner (8 outta 10 tits, vlogs should stick to scripts), and the insanely interesting Ayaan Hirsi Ali are all perfect examples of modern feminists who aren't Social Justice Warriors or so-called "progressives." While a vast majority of Social Justice feminists are busy writing and saying things that I can only liken to the wet touch of a dead fly, the women listed above remain sane faces of feminism, rather than adding to the pimple-speckled stains permeating the main movement's incarnation. I recommend looking into their writings.

Also, I'm completely sure that SJW-types are wondering why there are no men on my list of feminists who I seem to show "approval" towards. This reason may not make sense to you, but just because I do not fully agree with someone, that doesn't mean I do not like them nor believe they do not have important things to say. Moreover, I do not judge on the basis of sex, so excluding men from this list is in no way exemplary of my internalized misandry. Reread that caveat, and replace everything masculine to the feminine equivalent, and you will have a fun formula for how to phrase bullshit in an Orwellian SJW-style of Newspeak. As sad as it is to admit, I know far too much about this kind of nonsense. And before anyone accuses me of purposefully not acknowledging trans people, I'll take this moment to inform you that I regularly dream of having a threesome with Bailey Jay and Buck Angel, in the shower, covered in confetti and glitter with whistles in every orifice. That's not a justification, I just wanted to put that image in your head.

For a fun exercise, search the web for large feminist publications and read through their articles on "man-hating." It's kind of brilliant. They almost always take on a highly defensive or an unironically hateful nature, spouting out how men's problems have always been feminist issues, but then go out of their way to say that focusing only on the problems of women instead of those of men isn't in anyway a sign of their apathy, often drudging out 'ye old "Patriarchy hurts men too." The funniest ones make statements such as "Feminists don't hate men or the issues of men. But please, fellas, stop trying to make this about men." Basically: "Sure, we care, now do something for women."

I don't predict this trend of theirs to die off any time soon, mainly thanks to the lulzy internet-drama and rhetorical warfare between feminists and MRAs. There's almost nothing more hilarious than reading arguments between these two groups, especially once the subgroups get involved. Before I get too far ahead of myself, let's list some of these subgroups:

RadFem = Radical Feminist

SWERF = Sex Worker Exclusionary Radical Feminist

TERF = Trans-Exclusionary Radical Feminist

MRAs = Men's Rights Activists/Advocates

MGTOWs = Men Going Their Own Way

Right-o. Now here's a broad-brush

breakdown. Feminists hate RadFems, SWERFs, TERFs, MRAs and MGTOWs. RadFems hate MGTOWs, MRAs, feminists and TERFs. MRAs and MGTOWs are against the rest.

You will, of course, be able to find people who can fall into different groups or generally get along with others, but for the sake of preserving your sanity, let's pretend they don't exist for the time being.

Now, the typical beginnings of pro/anti-feminist arguments tend to follow specific patterns. This is the most common.

Content (article/video) --> Comment

Comment --> Disagreement(Reply #1)

Disagreement --> Accusation(Reply #2)

Accusation --> Argument

The accusation phase is what will be the deciding factor as to the argument's nature. The lines of contention can be as simple as "You're just another dumb MRA," or "Great, a feminazi." The moment this happens, people begin spouting what they believe or what group they belong to, quickly finding their uncommon ground and blabbering about one another. An MRA might raise an issue about circumcision, then the RadFem/SJW will tell the MRA to shut up about men because women have it worse.

Then a MGTOW will step in to inform us that women aren't worth the time of any man, stating that every woman wants to waste your time and take your hard-earned shekels to buy more **JEW**elry. Another MRA will agree, then a **NAWALT** will, of course, step in to say "**N**ot **A**ll **W**omen **A**re **L**ike **T**hat," adding nothing to the fun of the argument. And for good measure, Karen Straughan will probably show up with an essay, providing us with an all-Canadian dose of NobodyCares™(Right? Right? Right?).

And TotalBiscuit will probably leave a comment, for some reason. Spurious facts will spill out in all directions, and by this point somebody's already been called a whore, so the RadFems will complain about slut shaming, then somebody will mention their transition, causing an MRA or a TERF to say they're not a real man/woman, and the clusterfuck rolls along; thus completing the circle of (no)life.

The reason I bring up these groups is simple, and of course follows the theme of this section's name. Chances are that you have heard or maybe even have said that the rights of men have always been a part of feminism, and that the rights of men and women are viewed equally in the eyes of feminism. Today, this is blatantly false. If it were not, then "MRA" (Men's Rights Advocate/Activist) would not be used as an insult in feminist circles. Their contentions with MRAs would be that they use a name that isn't feminism, and then these two groups would make peace and work out whatever issues they see in the world. But of course, that most likely will not happen any time soon. Because if people are getting along and groups are cooperating, there are less people for Social Justice Warriors to claim they represent.

I won't say that I can predict the future, but allow me to make an educated guess. Should this little book of mine gain any sort of attention, you will undoubtedly find a review of it claiming that I am a sexist, hateful, bigoted, right-wing MRA. Somebody (most likely a darkie or a Jew) will probably make accusations of racism while they're at it. On the flip-side, even remotely suggesting that feminism has some good parts to it will send some MGTOW or another on a rant about how much of a cuckolded-dipshit beta-male bitch I am. It's in their nature.

So finally, with all that information out of the way, how does one approach Sargon's Law?

Keeping things as simple as they've been thus far, I have to say that it is rendered effectively wrong due to its massive generalization. It applies to a select few of these "progressive" feminists and SJWs, often only the ones who are fighting their way towards recognition, or lashing out during their downfall. No way for me to fake being nice about this, so I won't try.

Sargon's Law applies to SJWs who are either losing their "internet fame" or are seeking it. As would a wounded or confused animal, they attempt to strike in ways that they believe will deal some damage. But Social Justice Warriors and their feminist hosts exist in "safe spaces" and "hugboxes," where challenges, disagreements, dissension, skeptical inquiry and questions in general are shunned and removed. Strip these away from a person, and you are left with nothing but what makes them and their ideology operate. They become insular. Myopic. Closed.

If they want to hurt you, they do not know

how. They become forced to act on what would be harmful to *themselves*. If their existence is predicated on being perceived as a liberal, they will make attempts at "slandering" you as right-wing, winning social brownie points from their peers. If they are stridently atheist, they will try to make you out to be a back-woods, cousin-screwing, bible-thumping hillbilly. If they claim they do lots of "work" against racism, they will try to paint you as a racist through any means of mental gymnastics in the hopes of convincing others. If they are a radical feminist, they will say you "hate all women." If they are trans, they will not-so-subtly hint that you are transphobic.

As you have most likely noticed, this is a common tactic. One not limited to RadFems and SJWs. It's the old tried-and-true Ad Hominem fallacy. It is an attack on the individual, not a rebuttal or disproof of their opposing ideas. In essence, it is little more than a desperate plea to the audience. Sargon's Law can only apply to them when the accuser is projecting. This does not happen often. When it does, however, all it shows is that people can be hypocrites, and hypocrisies can bite you in the ass.

A self-described pedophile could insult people by calling them pedophiles. A racist could accuse others of racism. A fervent hater of men could accuse others of sexism. People who call themselves "inclusive" could hint at segregation being a good thing if it protects minorities from "white influences."

Sargon's Law is, at best, a fine starting point for when strange situations mix with strange individuals. As a law though, it is as broken as the people it applies to.

The Weight of Social Justice

If your reaction to Social Justice Warriors has been one of anger, annoyance or anything in between, then you're doing it wrong. Pity them. Feel sorry for them. They truly deserve it, because of what they have to carry. SJWs struggle with uplifting minority groups. SJWs champion every cause of every woman, everywhere. In these last few pages, I will leave you with a sad, sad truth about this ideology.

As much as I would love to lump all of the blame on my own generation, SJWs aren't simply a millennial phenomenon. It isn't just hipsters engaging in the lazy online "activism" that's become all too prevalent these days. No. Social Justice Warriors aren't "new" in any sense of the word.

You already know what these people embody, simply under a different name. The majority of Social Justice Warriors are outspoken, fairly wealthy, well connected... and white.

They are, by damn-near all indicators, an authoritarian reincarnation of The White Man's Burden. Their sole mission is to "elevate" the poor, oppressed, lowly, misunderstood masses of women and minorities and bring them up to the white man's level. Their principle's very core is predicated upon the soft bigotry of low expectations. This movement was far less powerful in the past, but it now benefits from society's collective political correctness and white guilt.

Whenever an injustice occurs, they will only speak of it if women or minorities are involved. If it does not suit the narrative, then it is to be ignored. But one of the reasons why they so heavily rely on manipulating language is because this framework is fragile.

Look no further than the sexual assaults which took place on New Year's in Cologne, Germany. Hundreds of minorities (a protected group) had sexually harassed and robbed women (a protected group) on a scale unseen since the dark ages. For a few days, there was utter silence. When news of this event became mainstream – despite efforts to suppress it – Social Justice journalists, bloggers, columnists and commentators lost their minds as a dagger tore the narrative apart.

The Young Turks spent nearly ten minutes discussing how racists and bigots will use the story to drum up Islamophobia, and that sexism is everywhere and the Catholic Church and U.S college campuses are proof of that.

Laurie Penny wrote an article for NewStatesman titled "After Cologne, we can't let the bigots steal feminism," in which she said this: "It'd be great if we could take rape, sexual assault and structural misogyny as seriously every day as we do when migrants and Muslims are involved as perpetrators..." and "It's a miracle! Finally, the right wing cares about rape culture!"

A protected group transgressed against another protected group, and condemning the actions of non-whites makes you racist. So they needed to change the topic. They needed to pick another enemy. Basically, "What some of the migrants did was awful and wrong, but look at the bad things white people have done in western countries. The right-wing only cares about misogyny when they can bash brown people, so now let's bash the right-wing and never speak of this again."

Regarding an incident like the sexual harassment in Cologne, the only viable Social Justice tactic was to go silent and wait for a white man or a right-winger to say something against immigration or to criticize Islam (Hello, Mr. Trump), allowing them to continue with the narrative of "White people are bad, y'all."

The duplicitous nature of The White Man's Burden is that the white man is evil, and the white man is here to save you. They must, at all times, be both enemy and ally. If it were otherwise, SJWs would be unable to convince people to put them in their ears, and endure the endless whispers.

For modern feminism to be viewed as srs business in the west again, it must first isolate this element, and cast it from the ranks. To those who remain unconvinced of SJWs being descend from the White Man's Burden, then consider my second theory: They are Chris-chan's spirit animal.

Finally, if you maintain that Social Justice is a force intended to do good, I will leave you with this:

"The road to hell is paved with good intentions."

P.S, Next time a Social Justice Warrior or a feminist criticizes how women are portrayed in "the media," tell them they just don't understand Jewish culture. It's fuckin' hilarious.

www.ingramcontent.com/pod-product-compliance
Lightning Source LLC
Chambersburg PA
CBHW062053280526
45788CB00003B/1215